D0115279

FOLLOWING JESUS

8 STUDIES FOR INDIVIDUALS OR GROUPS

Douglas Connelly

With Notes for Leaders

IVP Connect

An imprint of InterVarsity Press
Downers Grove, Illinois

InterVarsity Press
P.O. Box 1400, Downers Grove, IL 60515-1426
World Wide Web: www.ivpress.com
Email: email@ivpress.com

InterVarsity Press® is the book-publishing division of InterVarsity Christian Fellowship/USA®, a
movement of students and faculty active on campus at hundreds of universities, colleges and schools
of nursing in the United States of America, and a member movement of the International Fellowship
of Evangelical Students. For information about local and regional activities, write Public Relations
Dept., InterVarsity Christian Fellowship/USA, 6400 Schroeder Rd., P.O. Box 7895, Madison, WI
53707-7895, or visit the IVCF website at <www.intervarsity.org>.

LifeGuide® is a registered trademark of InterVarsity Christian Fellowship.

Cover image: breckeni/iStockphoto

ISBN 978-0-8308-3135-7

Printed in the United States of America ∞

InterVarsity Press is committed to protecting the environment and to the responsible
use of natural resources. As a member of Green Press Initiative we use recycled paper
whenever possible. To learn more about the Green Press Initiative, visit <www.
greenpressinitiative.org>.

| P | 18 | 17 | 16 | 15 | 14 | 13 | 12 | 11 | 10 | 9 | 8 | 7 | 6 | 5 | 4 | 3 | 2 | 1 |
| Y | 24 | 23 | 22 | 21 | 20 | 19 | 18 | 17 | 16 | 15 | 14 | 13 | 12 | 11 | 10 | 09 | | | |

Contents

Getting the Most Out of *Following Jesus*

The Christian life begins with a *step* of faith. We put our trust in Jesus as our Savior and Lord and King. In that instant we are made new and we pass from death to life. But that first step of faith leads to a *walk* of obedience and trust and holiness. The process begins with a decisive act, but we don't remain just inside the door of God's kingdom. We go on in our walk with the Lord. We grow up into spiritual maturity. We launch out on a journey through life toward an eternity in Christ's presence.

All the images I have just touched on are pictures the Bible uses to describe the life of a Christian—a walk, a journey, growing up, entering a kingdom. This study guide explores what it means to follow Jesus. It's an exciting, challenging adventure! The journey leads through hard places sometimes, but we have an incredible Helper, the Holy Spirit, who gives us the energy and the desire to press on.

I've designed this guide especially for new believers, but it will revitalize any Christian at any stage in their spiritual journey. It's not a self-help program but instead shows how the Holy Spirit will move us in new directions and give us new goals in life. Get ready to see some changes! The challenge of following Jesus never ends.

Suggestions for Individual Study

1. As you begin each study, pray that God will speak to you through his Word.

2. Read the introduction to the study and respond to the personal reflection question or exercise. This is designed to help you focus on God and on the theme of the study.

3. Each study deals with a particular passage so that you can delve into the author's meaning in that context. Read and reread the passage to be studied. The questions are written using the language of the New International Version, so you may wish to use that version of the Bible. The New Revised Standard Version is also recommended.

4. This is an inductive Bible study, designed to help you discover for yourself what Scripture is saying. The study includes three types of questions. *Observation* questions ask about the basic facts: who, what, when, where and how. *Interpretation* questions delve into the meaning of the passage. *Application* questions help you discover the implications of the text for growing in Christ. These three keys unlock the treasures of Scripture.

Write your answers to the questions in the spaces provided or in a personal journal. Writing can bring clarity and deeper understanding of yourself and of God's Word.

5. It might be good to have a Bible dictionary handy. Use it to look up any unfamiliar words, names or places.

6. Use the prayer suggestion to guide you in thanking God for what you have learned and to pray about the applications that have come to mind.

7. You may want to go on to the suggestion under "Now or Later," or you may want to use that idea for your next study.

Suggestions for Members of a Group Study

1. Come to the study prepared. Follow the suggestions for individual study mentioned above. You will find that careful preparation will greatly enrich your time spent in group discussion.

2. Be willing to participate in the discussion. The leader of your group will not be lecturing. Instead, he or she will be encouraging the members of the group to discuss what they have learned. The leader will be asking the questions that are found in this guide.

3. Stick to the topic being discussed. Your answers should be based on the verses which are the focus of the discussion and not on outside authorities such as commentaries or speakers. These studies focus on a particular passage of Scripture. Only rarely should you refer to other portions of the Bible. This allows for everyone to participate in in-depth study on equal ground.

4. Be sensitive to the other members of the group. Listen attentively when they describe what they have learned. You may be surprised by their insights! Each question assumes a variety of answers. Many questions do not have "right" answers, particularly questions that aim at meaning or application. Instead the questions push us to explore the passage more thoroughly.

When possible, link what you say to the comments of others. Also, be affirming whenever you can. This will encourage some of the more hesitant members of the group to participate.

5. Be careful not to dominate the discussion. We are sometimes so eager to express our thoughts that we leave too little opportunity for others to respond. By all means participate! But allow others to also.

6. Expect God to teach you through the passage being discussed and through the other members of the group. Pray that you will have an enjoyable and profitable time together, but also that as a result of the study you will find ways that you can take action individually and/or as a group.

7. Remember that anything said in the group is considered confidential and should not be discussed outside the group unless specific permission is given to do so.

8. If you are the group leader, you will find additional suggestions at the back of the guide.

1

Carrying a Cross

Following Jesus sounds like a wonderful adventure—and Jesus does promise a life of incredible challenge and enriching purpose as we follow him. But the satisfying path is not necessarily the easy path. Several times during his ministry Jesus urged his followers to consider the cost of following him. Salvation in Jesus is free—a gift of God's grace. Following Jesus as a faithful disciple, on the other hand, requires the willing sacrifice of all the things we hold most closely.

GROUP DISCUSSION. Have you ever volunteered for a job only to find out later that far more was being asked of you than you were originally told? Tell the group your story.

PERSONAL REFLECTION. Have you ever thought that being a Christian required too much from you? How would you counsel a friend who thought they were paying too high a price to follow Jesus?

Jesus and a large crowd of followers were making their way to Jerusalem. It's likely they came upon crosses standing along the road—crosses ready to be used if executions were needed. Jesus used that sobering symbol of death to call his followers to an all-consuming commitment to him. *Read Luke 14:25-35.*

1. What do you think of when you see a cross that is worn as a piece of jewelry or displayed in front of a church?

What do you think people in Jesus' day thought of when they saw a cross?

2. How does carrying a cross illustrate what is required to follow Jesus (v. 27)?

3. What do you think "hate" means in this passage?

What would be a modern-day example of how a Christian may be forced to "hate" his family or his own life (v. 26) in order to follow Jesus fully?

_____

4. How do you think the people listening to Jesus that day reacted to the demands he was making?

How do you react to Jesus' demands reading them now?

_____

5. What consequences result from not calculating the cost of building a tower or going to war (vv. 28-32)?

_____

6. What point about discipleship is Jesus trying to communicate by using these illustrations?

7. What is a Christian like who loses his or her "saltiness" (v. 34)?

8. Which of the costs of following Jesus fully seem especially high to you?

What is it about following Jesus that makes the cost or sacrifice worth it?

Consider what you are willing to sacrifice in order to follow Jesus fully. Express the level of your commitment to Jesus in prayer.

Now or Later

Check out a short biography about a Christian who sacrificed deeply to follow Jesus. Elisabeth Elliot's book *Through Gates of Splendor* is a classic; you could also search online for the story of John and Betty Stam or Bishop Polycarp, or watch the movie "Amazing Grace" about William Wilberforce. How did the person you learned about respond to the call of Jesus in their life?

2

Growing into Maturity

1 Peter 1:22—2:3

Our granddaughter Allison just turned nine years old. She's not the little baby we held so carefully or the bouncing toddler we helped to walk around the room. Instead of asking us to read a book to her, she reads to us! It's hard to see your children or grandchildren grow up, but it would be tragic if they remained children forever. We expect them to move steadily toward maturity and independence as an adult. We miss the joys of having a young child around but enter into new joys as we see them grow up.

GROUP DISCUSSION. What did you enjoy most about your childhood? What did you like least about being a child?

PERSONAL REFLECTION. In what areas did you have the most difficulty as you grew up? What would you identify as a continuing area of immaturity in your life?

Spiritual growth and maturity are just as important as growing up physically. It's easier, of course, to stay at the elementary levels of Christian growth; not much pain is involved and people don't expect much from you. But the Bible challenges us to grow beyond a foundational knowledge of Christian truth and beyond the initial experience with the Lord to the place of maturity and strength. The apostle Peter urges his Christian friends to break out of the spiritual nursery and to press toward adulthood. *Read 1 Peter 1:22—2:3.*

1. What evidence of genuine spiritual life does Peter see in these Christians (1:22)?

2. What does it mean to be "born again" or born anew (1:23)?

How do we receive that new birth according to Peter?

3. Would you say that you have had a new birth in Christ in your life? If you have, describe when and how that happened.

4. What do you learn about God's Word in 1:23-25?

Does any of Peter's testimony change your view of God's Word? Why or why not?

5. What is the "pure spiritual milk" that Peter urges us to crave (2:2)?

6. What will be the result of receiving this spiritual nourishment (2:2)?

7. Part of spiritual growth is putting off the remnants of the old life. Which of the old patterns in 1 Peter 2:1 are the most difficult for you to remove?

8. Where would you place yourself on the "craving scale" for God's truth if 10 represented "I can't go very long without it" and 1 represented "I can avoid it for weeks"?

What can you do to move yourself one or two notches higher on that scale—to increase your desire to hear, understand and obey God's Word to you?

---

9. How would you communicate the importance of God's Word in your life to a friend who doesn't know Jesus?

Pray that God would give you the strength to get rid of the remnants of your old life that you struggle with, and then ask him to deepen your desire to listen to his voice and obey his Word.

Now or Later

One way to stimulate a desire for God's Word is to pursue a regular Bible reading. You may want to start with one of the Gospels in the New Testament. Read one chapter of the Gospel of Mark, for example, each day. What is Jesus speaking to you about as you read? Talk to him about your desire to obey what God says. If you miss a day or two, don't quit. Go back to the pattern and listen to God speak.

3

Keeping in Step with the Spirit

I took a walk last winter in an orchard not far from my Michigan home. I'm not an expert on fruit trees, so I didn't have a clue what kind of fruit the bare trees normally produced. If I had returned to the orchard in the summer, however, I would have had no trouble identifying the trees. The fruit produced by the trees would have been hanging off every limb.

GROUP DISCUSSION. Tell the group what your favorite fruit is and how you most like to eat it. What would you need to grow the fruit yourself?

PERSONAL REFLECTION. If you could change one aspect of your personality, what would it be? Why would you want to change that particular aspect?

Before Jesus went back to heaven, he promised his disciples that he would send another helper to guide their lives and encourage their hearts—the Holy Spirit. Jesus still keeps that promise to his followers today. Following Jesus means that we live under the guidance and power of the Holy Spirit. The Spirit desires to produce the character of Jesus in every believer. Christlikeness doesn't just happen, however. We are called to keep our lives in step with the Spirit's direction. *Read Galatians 5:16-26.*

1. What does Paul identify as the primary conflict within every Christian?

Scan through this passage again and explain how that conflict flares up in a Christian's life.

2. Describe how the conflict between the sinful nature and the Spirit emerges in your own life.

How have you tried to resolve that conflict in the past?

3. In your opinion, which "acts of the sinful nature" listed in verses 19-21 are most prevalent in our culture?

Which of these acts seem to entangle you most often?

4. Why does Paul refer to the qualities in verses 22 and 23 as the "fruit" of the Spirit?

5. What spiritual fruit is most obvious in your life—and which is least obvious?

6. What specific practices can a Christian engage in to nurture the development of the fruit of the Spirit in his or her life?

7. If we have "crucified the sinful nature" (v. 24), why do we still sense a conflict between the sinful nature and the Holy Spirit (v. 17)?

---

8. In what ways can a Christian discern the Spirit's guidance in a situation or a decision?

---

9. What tends to distract you from keeping in step with the Spirit's direction?

---

10. Describe to the group one specific step that you will take this week to "crucify" the sinful nature and its desires and to live in the realm of God's Spirit. Ask the group to hold you accountable to do it.

Thank God for the Spirit's work in your life—and ask him to help you in the areas where you feel out of step with him.

Now or Later

Talk to someone in your church or Christian fellowship in whom you see the mature fruit of the Spirit. Ask that person how they discern the Spirit's direction in their life. Seek to implement some of their wisdom into your own journey with the Lord.

4

Running the Race

I started the race so well! At the 100-meter mark I was ahead of every other sixth-grade boy. At 200 meters I was still out in front but was fading fast. The problem was not my speed; the problem was the length of the race. I finally crossed the finish line but at the back of the pack. "That's a big mistake most inexperienced runners make," my teacher, Mr. Johnson, explained as he walked with me back to the school. "They have a lot of energy and run fast at first, but they have no endurance for the long haul."

GROUP DISCUSSION. What "race" do you remember participating in—a gunnysack race, a three-legged race, a schoolyard challenge, an Olympic tryout? Did you win, fall down or choke?

PERSONAL REFLECTION. At what stage in a project do you tend to lose energy—halfway through, almost done, before it starts? Reflect on your endurance record.

The apostle Paul was a sports fanatic. If he were on earth today, he would love the World Cup soccer matches, the Stanley Cup playoffs and the Super Bowl. Most of all he would love those feats of strength and endurance we call the Olympic Games. Paul would enjoy the thrill of it all but he would also see in the athlete's performance a powerful example of what it means to follow Jesus. *Read 1 Corinthians 9:19-27.*

---

1. What comparisons can you think of between a race and the Christian life?

Do you personally find it to be a helpful comparison? Why or why not?

---

2. Paul explains his motivation for running the race in verses 19-23. What present-day examples might be substituted for the groups Paul was burdened to reach with the message of Jesus?

---

3. Does "becoming all things to all people" (see v. 22) mean we participate in their sinful behavior? Explain your answer.

4. What is "the prize" Paul challenges us to run for (vv. 24-25)?

5. Do you think of gaining a prize or reward when you serve the Lord in some way? Why or why not?

6. What may be involved in the "strict training" (v. 25) of an athlete and how does that apply to the Christian race?

7. In verses 26 and 27 Paul switches from the image of running to the sport of boxing. How does this new picture broaden your understanding of what it means to follow Jesus?

8. What might disqualify an athlete from winning the prize?

What might disqualify a Christian from gaining the prize?

---

9. How would you honestly describe your personal fitness for the Christian race: have never really started? too out of shape to run? getting my second wind? feeling like I could run forever? ready to drop out?

If you are falling behind, what will it cost in your life to get back in the race, running for the prize?

Pray that God would help you to focus your life on Jesus and on pleasing him. Pray also that he would give you not only a passion to run the Christian race but also endurance to finish well.

Now or Later

As a group, think about or talk about people in your community who are not being reached very effectively with the gospel: the poor, an immigrant population, latchkey kids, the elderly. How can you apply the principles of 1 Corinthians 9:19-23 and begin to reach one of these groups? What are your fears? What might be the rewards of such a commitment?

5

Constructing a Building

When my son Kyle wanted a fort for the backyard, my dad and I decided to build something that would stand up to hard play. After a couple weeks of work and several midcourse corrections, we finished a log fort that would light up any young boy's eyes. Last week we went past the house where the fort was first built. Four children now live there and the log fort still stands. I expect it will capture the imaginations of a few more generations of kids before it is torn down.

GROUP DISCUSSION. Tell the group about your most memorable "construction" project. It might be building a flowerbed, trying your hand at home improvement or constructing a science fair project.

PERSONAL REFLECTION. In what way is life like a building project? What "foundation" does your life rest upon?

The Bible uses the image of "building" to illustrate what it means to follow Jesus. Not only are we all involved in the project, but we will also all face an evaluation some day for our personal contribution. *Read 1 Corinthians 3:10-15.*

1. What kind of "building" is Paul talking about in this passage?

What helped you draw that conclusion?

2. How does it make you feel to think that you are one of the craftsmen working on God's building?

3. Jesus Christ is the foundation of God's building. How did Paul and the other early Christian leaders lay that foundation?

Why is this foundation so important for God's building?

4. When and how was the foundation of faith in Christ laid in your life, and who were the people responsible for laying it?

5. What does Paul mean when he talks about building with gold, silver or costly stones?

What about wood, hay or straw?

6. Paul refers in verse 13 to a "Day" of evaluation that all believers will face. What will Jesus be examining on that Day?

7. If our building survives the fire of Jesus' evaluation, we will receive a reward from him (v. 14). How do you envision that reward?

8. What will it mean to suffer loss of his reward (v. 15)?

9. Does this future Day of evaluation make you nervous or do you look forward to it with anticipation? Explain your answer.

Sit in silence for a few moments, asking the Lord to evaluate the quality of your work on his building right now. Then talk to him about what you sense him saying, and ask him to give you the courage to build in such a way that he is pleased.

Now or Later

Plan as a group to do something to build up God's building. Help a senior adult with yard work, prepare a meal for a needy family, baby-sit for a young couple, buy clothes or toys for a family shelter. Do it in Jesus' name, not for praise from others.

6

Fighting the Battle

Ephesians 6:10-18

Recently our church honored our two World War II veterans. As these men shared their stories about the assignments they had been given and the situations they had faced, we could almost see them as young GIs on a transit ship steaming across the ocean. The battles of that war changed their lives—and their generation.

GROUP DISCUSSION. Imagine yourself preparing for battle. What three things would you most want to take with you?

PERSONAL REFLECTION. Do you ever sense that you are struggling against forces that are not physical? What is the source of that opposition in your life?

The Bible makes it clear that the Christian experience can be like a battle. Powerful spiritual forces are set against us and are determined to defeat or discourage us from following the Lord.

We can't avoid the battle but we can take advantage of the spiritual protection God supplies. *Read Ephesians 6:10-18.*

---

1. Summarize what this passage tells you about the reality and nature of evil forces outside the realm of our sight or touch.

---

2. How have you as a believer experienced this ongoing struggle against "the spiritual forces of evil" in your own life?

---

3. Based on this passage, how strong are Satan and his demons?

What words and phrases reveal this?

---

4. How confident do you feel personally about facing Satan and his demons and why?

5. Four times in verses 10-14 Paul challenges us to stand our ground against Satan's attacks. What might make a believer vulnerable to the enemy and in danger of falling when attacked?

---

6. If the battle is a "spiritual" one, what does that tell you about the nature of the armor God provides?

What is our responsibility in regard to that armor?

---

7. What area of life might each piece of God's armor protect or be used for?

Belt of truth:

Breastplate of righteousness:

Footwear of peace:

Shield of faith:

Helmet of salvation:

Sword of the Spirit:

8. In what way is prayer a resource in the spiritual battle (v. 18)?

---

9. Which piece of armor do you need to "put on" more consistently in your life and why?

Ask God to help you be more aware of the spiritual forces standing against you—and more prepared to meet the enemy's attack.

Now or Later

Think of a friend, Christian leader or missionary who may be under spiritual attack. Pray for God's protection for that person. If possible, contact them and tell them you are praying specifically for strength against the enemy.

7

Becoming a Servant

Our culture doesn't put much value on serving. We are much more impressed with fame or acclaim. No reality television producers are searching the land for "the next American servant." Even in Christian circles, we tend to elevate the superstar preachers and the megahit musicians. Faithful men and women serving in small churches or visiting hospice patients don't get much notice.

GROUP DISCUSSION. Who would you nominate for the "servant of the year" award in your family or circle of friends for their selfless, compassionate service?

PERSONAL REFLECTION. Do you find it easier to serve or to be served? Think of a recent example of selfless service. Did you give it or receive it?

Jesus made it clear that, in his kingdom, serving others is the key to exaltation. He told his disciples that he had not come to earth to be served but to serve (Matthew 20:28). Those weren't just empty words either. Jesus consistently modeled that spirit of humility—even if it meant washing twelve pairs of dirty feet. *Read John 13:1-17.*

1. Imagine that you were one of the disciples in the room that night. What moods or emotions do you think were present as the evening unfolded?

How do you think you personally would have felt and responded as Jesus began to wash your feet?

2. Why do you think the disciples didn't wash the dust from their own feet as they entered this house?

3. What did Jesus know that the disciples did not know (vv. 1, 3, 11)?

Why does Jesus' knowledge make his act of washing their feet even more impressive?

4. What do you think Jesus' motives were in washing his disciples' feet?

5. How would you explain Peter's reaction to Jesus in verses 6 and 8?

Why did he eventually allow Jesus to wash his feet (see vv. 8, 10)?

6. How does Jesus expect his disciples (then and now) to follow his example (vv. 12-16)?

Does Jesus' command to "wash one another's feet" mean that the CEO of a company will be sorting mail and sharpening pencils for the employees? Explain your answer.

---

7. Imagine what Jesus might say to you if he bent to wash your feet today. What words of affirmation and blessing might you hear?

What words of evaluation or direction?

---

8. How will you put Jesus' teaching about servanthood into action in at least one relationship this week in your church, your workplace or your family?

Who can you ask to hold you accountable to carry through on your commitment?

*Pray that Jesus would make your heart like his by giving you a
deeper desire to serve others.*

Now or Later

You may want to close your group session with an actual foot
washing. One suggestion is for each person to wash the feet
of the person to his or her right and then have that person
wash the feet of the next person. If your group consists of mar-
ried couples, you could also have spouses wash each other's
feet. Or you may want to separate into two groups—males and
females—for foot washing. In any case, after each washing, the
person washing speaks words of encouragement and blessing
to the one whose feet have been washed. You will need basins,
water, towels—and humility! This can be a very moving experience for a small group.

8

Entering a Kingdom

Hebrews 12:14-29

I have family friends who are missionaries in a Third World country. What frustrates them the most is not ministry in a difficult place, but the difficulty of daily life. The system of government in that nation seems to be built on corruption, bribery, threats and constantly changing regulations. Sometimes it takes a whole day just to get a driver's license renewed or to obtain a building permit for a new fence. Sharing the message of the gospel is challenging enough in that culture, but the actual living in such a dysfunctional "kingdom" can be very disheartening.

GROUP DISCUSSION. If you could choose to live anywhere in the world for a year, what issues would be most important in your choice? Culture? Climate? Available activities? Government?

PERSONAL REFLECTION. What do you like best about the national government you live under? What aspects of the government would you like to change?

When Jesus began his ministry, he announced that the arrival of God's kingdom was near. Christians are in the process of receiving that kingdom as Jesus rules in our lives as king. *Read Hebrews 12:14-29.*

---

1. What indications can you glean from verses 14-17 about what it means "to be holy"?

---

2. What effort do you make to live at peace with all (v. 14)?

---

3. Create a chart that compares the experiences of those who received the law at Mount Sinai (vv. 18-21) with the privileges of those who have received God's grace in Jesus (vv. 22-24).

Which side of the chart more closely reflects your experience and view of God?

_____

4. No matter which side of the chart you identify with more, what do you think would help you learn to enjoy the privileges of grace more deeply in your own life?

_____

5. What aspects of the description of heaven in verses 22-24 make you most excited about living there forever and why?

_____

6. Why does the writer add the warning of verses 25-27 when he has just emphasized the blessings of verses 22-24?

7. What are the benefits of living as a citizen of "a kingdom that cannot be shaken" rather than simply as a citizen of a world that God will shake once more in the future (vv. 27-28)?

8. In light of vv. 28-29, share with each other one benefit of his kingdom you've experienced this week. Begin with the phrase "I praise God for his . . ."

9. How should the fact that "our 'God is a consuming fire'" affect our attitude toward him in worship?

How should it affect our attitude toward his Word, the Bible?

10. As you think back through the biblical images of following Jesus that we have studied in this guide, which image has affected you most deeply? Explain how it has strengthened your commitment to Christ.

Ask God to help you focus on living as a citizen of Christ's kingdom rather than simply as a citizen of a shaky world.

Now or Later

Conclude your study with a time of reverent worship to God. Singing worship songs focused on God's holy character might be a good way to begin. Expressing praise to God for his grace and his goodness might be another element to include. Even our body position in worship (standing, kneeling, etc.) can express the attitude of our hearts before the Lord. Try to envision your worship joined with millions of angels and millions of believers made perfect in heaven. Try to keep that perspective as you worship with your fellow Christians in church. Exalt God as the ruler over all and Jesus as the one who bridges the gap between sinful humanity and a holy God.

Leader's Notes

MY GRACE IS SUFFICIENT FOR YOU. (2 COR 12:9)

Leading a Bible discussion can be an enjoyable and rewarding experience. But it can also be *scary*—especially if you've never done it before. If this is your feeling, you're in good company. When God asked Moses to lead the Israelites out of Egypt, he replied, "O Lord, please send someone else to do it!" (Ex 4:13). It was the same with Solomon, Jeremiah and Timothy, but God helped these people in spite of their weaknesses, and he will help you as well.

You don't need to be an expert on the Bible or a trained teacher to lead a Bible discussion. The idea behind these inductive studies is that the leader guides group members to discover for themselves what the Bible has to say. This method of learning will allow group members to remember much more of what is said than a lecture would.

These studies are designed to be led easily. As a matter of fact, the flow of questions through the passage from observation to interpretation to application is so natural that you may feel that the studies lead themselves. This study guide is also flexible. You can use it with a variety of groups—student, professional, neighborhood or church groups. Each study takes forty-five to sixty minutes in a group setting.

There are some important facts to know about group dynamics and encouraging discussion. The suggestions listed below should enable you to effectively and enjoyably fulfill your role as leader.

Preparing for the Study

1. Ask God to help you understand and apply the passage in your own life. Unless this happens, you will not be prepared to lead others. Pray too for the various members of the group. Ask God to open your hearts to the message of his Word and motivate you to action.

2. Read the introduction to the entire guide to get an overview of the entire book and the issues which will be explored.

3. As you begin each study, read and reread the assigned Bible passage to familiarize yourself with it.

4. This study guide is based on the New International Version of the Bible. It will help you and the group if you use this translation as the basis for your study and discussion.

5. Carefully work through each question in the study. Spend time in meditation and reflection as you consider how to respond.

6. Write your thoughts and responses in the space provided in the study guide. This will help you to express your understanding of the passage clearly.

7. It might help to have a Bible dictionary handy. Use it to look up any unfamiliar words, names or places. (For additional help on how to study a passage, see chapter five of *How to Lead a LifeGuide Bible Study*, InterVarsity Press.)

8. Consider how you can apply the Scripture to your life. Remember that the group will follow your lead in responding to the studies. They will not go any deeper than you do.

9. Once you have finished your own study of the passage, familiarize yourself with the leader's notes for the study you are leading. These are designed to help you in several ways. First, they tell you the purpose the study guide author had in mind when writing the study. Take time to think through how the study questions work together to accomplish that purpose. Second, the notes provide you with additional background information or suggestions on group dynamics for various questions. This information can be useful when people have difficulty understanding or answering a question. Third, the leader's notes can alert you to potential problems you may encounter during the study.

10. If you wish to remind yourself of anything mentioned in the leader's notes, make a note to yourself below that question in the study.

Leading the Study

1. Begin the study on time. Open with prayer, asking God to help the group to understand and apply the passage.

2. Be sure that everyone in your group has a study guide. Encourage the group to prepare beforehand for each discussion by reading the introduction to the guide and by working through the questions in the study.

3. At the beginning of your first time together, explain that these studies are meant to be discussions, not lectures. Encourage the members of the group to participate. However, do not put pressure on those who may be hesitant to speak during the first few sessions. You may want to suggest the following guidelines to your group.

☐ Stick to the topic being discussed.

☐ Your responses should be based on the verses which are the focus of the discussion and not on outside authorities such as commentaries or speakers.

☐ These studies focus on a particular passage of Scripture. Only rarely should you refer to other portions of the Bible. This allows for everyone to participate in in-depth study on equal ground.

☐ Anything said in the group is considered confidential and will not be discussed outside the group unless specific permission is given to do so.

☐ We will listen attentively to each other and provide time for each person present to talk.

☐ We will pray for each other.

4. Have a group member read the introduction at the beginning of the discussion.

5. Every session begins with a group discussion question. The question or activity is meant to be used before the passage is read. The question introduces the theme of the study and encourages group members to begin to open up. Encourage as many members as possible to participate, and be ready to get the discussion going with your own response.

This section is designed to reveal where our thoughts or feelings need to be transformed by Scripture. That is why it is especially important not to read the passage before the discussion question is asked. The passage will tend to color the honest reactions people would otherwise give because they are, of course, supposed to think the way the Bible does.

You may want to supplement the group discussion question with an icebreaker to help people to get comfortable. See the community section of *Small Group Idea Book* for more ideas.

You also might want to use the personal reflection question with your group. Either allow a time of silence for people to respond individually or discuss it together.

6. Have a group member (or members if the passage is long) read aloud the passage to be studied. Then give people several minutes to read the passage again silently so that they can take it all in.

7. Question 1 will generally be an overview question designed to briefly survey the passage. Encourage the group to look at the whole passage, but try to avoid getting sidetracked by questions or issues that will be addressed later in the study.

8. As you ask the questions, keep in mind that they are designed to be used just as they are written. You may simply read them aloud. Or you may prefer to express them in your own words.

There may be times when it is appropriate to deviate from the study guide. For example, a question may have already been answered. If so, move on to the next question. Or someone may raise an important question not covered in the guide. Take time to discuss it, but try to keep the group from going off on tangents.

9. Avoid answering your own questions. If necessary, repeat or rephrase them until they are clearly understood. Or point out something you read in the leader's notes to clarify the context or meaning. An eager group quickly becomes passive and silent if they think the leader will do most of the talking.

10. Don't be afraid of silence. People may need time to think about the question before formulating their answers.

11. Don't be content with just one answer. Ask, "What do the rest of you think?" or "Anything else?" until several people have given answers to the question.

12. Acknowledge all contributions. Try to be affirming whenever possible. Never reject an answer. If it is clearly off-base, ask, "Which verse led you to that conclusion?" or again, "What do the rest of you think?"

13. Don't expect every answer to be addressed to you, even though this will probably happen at first. As group members become more at ease, they will begin to truly interact with each other. This is one sign of healthy discussion.

14. Don't be afraid of controversy. It can be very stimulating. If you don't resolve an issue completely, don't be frustrated. Move on and keep it in mind for later. A subsequent study may solve the problem.

15. Periodically summarize what the group has said about the passage. This helps to draw together the various ideas mentioned and gives continuity to the study. But don't preach.

16. At the end of the Bible discussion you may want to allow group members a time of quiet to work on an idea under "Now or Later." Then discuss what you experienced. Or you may want to encourage group members to work on these ideas between meetings. Give an opportunity

during the session for people to talk about what they are learning.

17. Conclude your time together with conversational prayer, adapting the prayer suggestion at the end of the study to your group. Ask for God's help in following through on the commitments you've made.

18. End on time.

Many more suggestions and helps are found in *How to Lead a LifeGuide Bible Study.*

Components of Small Groups

A healthy small group should do more than study the Bible. There are four components to consider as you structure your time together.

Nurture. Small groups help us to grow in our knowledge and love of God. Bible study is the key to making this happen and is the foundation of your small group.

Community. Small groups are a great place to develop deep friend-ships with other Christians. Allow time for informal interaction before and after each study. Plan activities and games that will help you get to know each other. Spend time having fun together going on a picnic or cooking dinner together.

Worship and prayer. Your study will be enhanced by spending time praising God together in prayer or song. Pray for each other's needs and keep track of how God is answering prayer in your group. Ask God to help you to apply what you are learning in your study.

Outreach. Reaching out to others can be a practical way of apply-ing what you are learning, and it will keep your group from becoming self-focused. Host a series of evangelistic discussions for your friends or neighbors. Clean up the yard of an elderly friend. Serve at a soup kitchen together, or spend a day working on a Habitat house.

Many more suggestions and helps in each of these areas are found in *Small Group Idea Book.* Information on building a small group can be found in *Small Group Leaders' Handbook* and *The Big Book on Small Groups* (both from InterVarsity Press). Reading through one of these books would be worth your time.

Study 1. Carrying a Cross. Luke 14:25-35.

Purpose: To challenge us to consider the cost of following Jesus.

Opening paragraphs. The leader needs to remind the study group (probably more than once) that in this passage Jesus is not talking about a person's initial commitment of faith in Jesus. He is laying down the requirements for discipleship. We are made children of God by faith alone, but Jesus also calls believers to the path of discipleship. Some believers make a commitment to discipleship only to fall away when the demands get difficult. Other believers understand the call to discipleship but do not respond obediently. Jesus wants us to consider the sacrifice ahead of time. The goal of this study guide is to move believers to new levels of devotion and obedience to Christ.

Obviously, nothing in the text itself says that Jesus and his fellow-travelers actually saw a cross as Jesus spoke, but it was not unusual for crosses to be left in public places of execution. The cross and the process of execution by crucifixion would have been familiar to every person in Jesus' audience.

Question 1. To Christians today, the cross has become a symbol of Christ's great love for us and his sacrifice for us. To people in Jesus' day, carrying a cross was a symbol of certain death. We've lost the sense of shock that first-century Christians felt when Jesus called them to pick up a cross and follow him.

Question 2. Following Jesus as a fully committed disciple involves dying to our own personal desires and plans and being willing to go and do whatever God leads us to. Taking up the cross implies that we willingly sacrifice everything, even our own lives if need be, to respond to Jesus' call. To follow Jesus means to accept the path of suffering because the world will hate the committed Christian as certainly as they hated Jesus.

Question 3. Jesus is not asking us to loathe our parents or our families. He uses the word *hate* with the sense of making a choice or having the place of first priority. Jesus is always to have the place of prominence in our lives. If it comes to a choice between obeying Jesus or fulfilling the desires of our families, Jesus is to be our first love.

A contemporary example might be a Christian choosing to go to seminary to be a pastor rather than accepting a position in the family business. In times of persecution Christians may be forced to sacrifice their own lives or their family's lives rather than renounce allegiance to Jesus. In one of the churches I pastored, a young man from Pakistan gave his life to Jesus. When it came time to return to his home country, he told me that very difficult times were ahead for him. I've never heard from the man since.

Question 5. The tower in Jesus' illustration is probably a watchtower, built to protect a vineyard or private estate, not a public tower or a tower in a city wall. Towers on a farm or in a vineyard might include a barn where crops or tools are stored. A person does not build such a structure unless he has calculated the cost. Otherwise the building is left unfinished and the owner becomes the object of ridicule.

Going to war is an even greater challenge. Lack of troops or supplies or weapons will bring humiliating defeat and disgrace.

Question 6. Jesus is trying to get his hearers to realize that a believer who wants to commit to the path of being Jesus' disciple must clearly calculate the cost of that decision in terms of personal sacrifice. We may think that decision is an easy one in the emotion of the moment, but Jesus wants us to make the decision only with sober reflection and consideration.

Question 7. In the region of Judea, most salt came from evaporated pools around the Dead Sea. The salt was mixed with gypsum and other impurities. If salt sat too long, the moisture in the air evaporated the genuine salt and left only the impurities. The salt lost its saltiness. A Christian who focuses only on possessions or on personal desires loses his or her effectiveness as a follower of Jesus. Their ability to create spiritual thirst in others or to season and preserve the culture (both functions of salt) is lost.

Question 8. Following Jesus requires great sacrifice but the rewards are abundant and eternal. The faithful follower experiences the peace of God even in difficult times. The disciple faces life with a sense of purpose. Whatever the follower of Jesus "gives up" in sacrifice is restored in the fellowship of God's family. Plus the faithful follower has heaven ahead and Jesus' approval on his or her life. The world competes for rewards that will perish while the faithful Christian receives rewards that last forever.

Study 2. Growing into Maturity. 1 Peter 1:22—2:3.
Purpose: To encourage us to desire and pursue spiritual growth.

Question 1. The readers of Peter's letter were already "obeying the truth" that the apostle had taught them, and were demonstrating "sincere love" for each other. These Christians had started well. They were "purified" by faith and were interested in growing spiritually. Peter encourages them to build on the spiritual foundation already evident in their lives.

Questions 2-3. These questions provide an opportunity for you to establish whether the members of the group have had a genuine faith encounter with Jesus Christ. Peter was confident that his readers had been born again. They had been made new by faith in Jesus as Savior and Lord. New birth comes to us as we believe and receive God's message of salvation, "the living and enduring word of God." Question 3 is not designed to embarrass the responders but to give them the opportunity to express their faith in front of the entire group.

Question 4. Peter wanted these growing Christians to have absolute confidence in God's truth. God's written Word, the Bible, is not just what God has spoken in the past; God is still speaking in his Word today to those who are willing to listen. The group's response to the second part of the question may not be a *change* in their view. Peter's testimony may simply *affirm* or *strengthen* the view they already have.

Question 5. Most interpreters of 1 Peter believe the "spiritual milk" in 2:2 is connected with the Word of God discussed at the end of chapter 1. These Christians, then, are urged to cultivate a desire for God's truth in their lives. Some students of 1 Peter, however, believe the term *milk* has a broader reference to all the elements of grace that God supplies—his Word, prayer, worship, fellowship with other believers. We are to crave all of these sources of spiritual nourishment, as all will lead to spiritual growth.

Question 6. Receiving spiritual nourishment promotes spiritual development and maturity. But even when we reach maturity, we can't ignore spiritual milk. It sustains our life in Christ—and keeps us growing. There is always more to learn in Christ, and more ways to grow in our knowledge and experience of him.

Question 7. This opinion question is designed to prompt the members of the group to talk about some areas of struggle they may be having. Listen without judgment. Encourage the entire group to be intentional in putting aside these rags of the old life.

Question 8. Making a list of the suggestions for growth on a white board might give even more ideas to members of the group. One possible way to increase their desire for God's truth is to implement the "Now or Later" suggestion for daily Bible reading. Your closing prayer as the leader could also be that God will strengthen each person's desire to hear and obey God's Word.

Study 3. Keeping in Step with the Spirit. Galatians 5:16-26.

Purpose: To open our lives to and learn to cooperate with the work of God's Spirit in producing Christlike character in us.

Question 1. Paul's emphasis is on the conflict within the Christian between the Holy Spirit and the resident power of sin in our bodies. The Holy Spirit indwells us when we believe on Jesus. His desire is to transform our character. We have been made new creatures in Christ, but the power of the old nature (called "the flesh" in some translations of the New Testament) pulls at us to return to the actions of the old life. This struggle between the Spirit and the sinful nature continues to rage in the believer. Becoming Christlike or Spirit-filled involves yielding ourselves to the Holy Spirit's gentle direction rather than to the demands of the sinful nature. The process of sanctification in the believer's life involves becoming more and more set apart to God and less and less marked by the actions and attitudes of the sinful nature.

Question 2. The responses to this question should not be judged. Let each person respond openly. Don't force any who are reluctant to respond.

Question 3. The first part of this question asks for an opinion. Again, give people a chance to express their opinions without correction or judgment.

This second question moves into some very personal areas. You may want to simply say that each person will have his or her own struggle and go to the next question. Or, you as the leader of the group may want to be the first to give your answer and then let any others speak who desire to give their answers. Don't let the responses get too detailed but give opportunity for honest expression.

Question 4. The fruit produced by a tree or vine expresses the true nature of the plant. An apple tree will not produce grapes. The "tree" (the Christian's life) should produce the "fruit" (observable character) that reflects his or her true nature. If we are being directed by God's Spirit, our lives should give observable evidence of his presence. Hanging from the limbs of our lives should be marks of the character of Christ.

Question 5. Try to listen to the responses without judgment or correction. The question asks for *self*-evaluation, not the evaluation of the group.

Question 6. Spiritual growth and the cultivation of the fruit of the Spirit are not automatic. We make choices. For example, we may choose to display the new attitudes of our new life in Christ in a difficult situation at work *or* we may fall back on the old attitudes and responses of the past. When we choose to act in the new way, the Holy Spirit gives us the power to carry through. When it comes to activities, we make choices too. Are we going to do the things and go to the places that characterized the old life or are we going to choose to follow the Spirit's prompting to do the things that mark us out as new creatures? The Holy Spirit will give us direction if we rely on his leading and listen to his voice, but he will not force his will on us.

Specific practices that help us cultivate the new life are reading God's Word with a desire to obey, spending time in prayer (talking *and* listening), developing relationships with other Christians, serving in areas of ministry, being mentored by a more mature Christian and worshiping with other believers.

Question 7. There is a sense in which the old nature was put to death when we believed on Jesus. We were made new in Christ. But the remnants of the old life still hang on while we are in these bodies. Those tattered fragments of the old life (called "the flesh" in some versions of the Bible) can be very powerful *if* we yield to their desires. The conflict we sense as Christians is between the old desires of the old life and the Spirit's desires that we walk as new creatures.

Question 8. We learn how to follow the Spirit primarily through the instruction of God's Word, the Bible. We also discern his direction in our lives through his inner witness to our spirit and through the wisdom and example of other believers. We can pray for the wisdom of the Spirit and then in faith believe that he gives us what we ask for.

Question 9. Christians tend to be distracted from following the Spirit when we stop listening to his direction and become more focused on our own desires. Cultivating a sensitive heart to the Spirit's gentle nudge or his quiet whisper is a key part of keeping in step with him. Either plunging ahead or lagging behind the Spirit's direction can bring confusion and conflict.

Question 10. Help to make each person's goal clear and reachable. "I will start acting like Jesus" is admirable but unreachable. In what setting or relationship do you need to act like Jesus? In what specific ways do you need to change? How will you remind yourself to do it? What part will the Holy Spirit play in changing you?

Study 4. Running the Race. 1 Corinthians 9:19-27.

Purpose: To grasp the importance of endurance in our commitment to Jesus.

Question 1. The Christian life, like a race, involves determination, training, discipline and endurance. Christians keep their eyes on one goal—to please Christ.

The image of a footrace bothers some people because of the element of competition. It sounds like we are trying to win over other Christians who lose. But the only competition Paul points to is winning the prize, the reward offered by Christ to those who faithfully follow him. Each of us can win the prize.

Emphasize with the group, though, that Paul is not talking about "winning" or earning our salvation. He is talking about receiving rewards from the Lord for our faithfulness to him in this life. Even the idea of rewards may bother some Christians, but Paul did not hesitate to strive for the crowns that Christ graciously offers to all who endure in their commitment and obedience to the Lord.

Questions 2-3. The group may list several categories of people who seem outside the normal realms of Christian evangelism: homosexuals, atheists, convicted criminals. Certainly Paul was not advocating participation in their behavior in order to win them to Christ. He was encouraging Christians to be willing to make an effort at genuine friendship and then to use that relationship as a platform for presenting the message of Jesus to them.

Question 4. The prize that the Lord offers is a reward for faithful service to him. The Bible sometimes calls these rewards "crowns." They are visible symbols of a believer's devotion and obedience to Christ during his or her life on earth. Those who serve Jesus with sincere motives and a desire to please him will receive a mark of their faithfulness that will be worn forever.

Question 6. An athlete must discipline his or her mind and body to focus only on the goal. The Christian needs the same discipline to fully follow Jesus and to keep their focus on pleasing Christ in all things. This life is not a practice run; it's the real thing—and we are to pay the price required to win the prize.

Some examples of the "strict training" are giving up "good" things in order to focus on what is most important, continuing the disciplines of training even when we get tired, putting aside any habits or practices that might hinder our pursuit of the prize, and cultivating an attitude that motivates us forward.

Question 7. Just like a runner disciplines herself to win, a boxer puts himself through a strict program of exercise, diet and training. The image of boxing focuses even more on bringing our desires under control so that we are prepared and strong for whatever an opponent may throw against us. The runner competes for the prize; the boxer must be ready to face an enemy who seeks to defeat him.

Question 8. An athlete might lose their prize if they cheat in some way or take a drug that gives them an unfair advantage. At our future evaluation before Christ, every hidden thing will be revealed. Our motives, our methods, our secret thoughts and hidden agendas will all be exposed. If anything impure or dishonest is revealed, we may be disqualified from receiving the reward Christ offers. It's important to remind the group that Paul is talking about a reward for faithful service, *not* salvation. Being disqualified will lead to a loss of reward, not the loss of salvation. We are saved by God's grace alone, not by our works.

Question 9. Let group members express themselves candidly without judgment. Help each person craft a plan to get back into the race of living wholeheartedly to please Christ and to gain his commendation on a life lived for his glory. Some members may say that they are doing well in their race. Encourage them to a new level of commitment and endurance.

Study 5. Constructing a Building. 1 Corinthians 3:10-15.

Purpose: To prompt us to examine how we are using our time, resources and energy to serve Jesus and to build God's kingdom.

Question 1. It's obvious that Paul is *not* talking about a literal building in this passage. Paul wants the Corinthians (and us) to see themselves as a diverse group of people with different skills and gifts, coming together to build a spiritual building. Every Christian is building God's building, the church. We aren't using literal bricks and mortar, but we are building into the lives of people through our ministries of love and encouragement or teaching or helping. As each member contributes to the project, the building grows stronger and larger and more beautiful. Paul's point is that we are *all* building. Some are building poorly and some are building well.

Question 2. Paul makes it clear that every Christian is building, whether we know it or not and whether we like it or not. We can't just sit on the side and refuse to build. The spiritual community of believers is being built every day in every life. That fact should make us feel honored but it can also bring a sense of apprehension. Let each group member express his or her feelings without correction or judgment from the leader or from others in the group.

Question 3. As the founder of the Corinthian church, Paul laid the spiritual foundation of the "building" by preaching the message of Jesus. These believers had heard the gospel and they had been taught the foundational truths of the Christian faith. It is on that foundation that any true work for God is built.

The foundation is important because our faith rests on Jesus' death and resurrection. Our ministries as Christians spring from what God has done in our lives by his grace. If the "building" we are working on stands on the wrong foundation, it will ultimately collapse.

Question 5. Most of the materials Paul lists are not building materials at all. Wood certainly qualifies, but who builds a house with gold— or with straw? The materials represent the quality and motives of each worker. Some Christians are excellent builders on God's building and they use exceptional materials. Other Christians rely on faulty methods and poor-quality materials. Some works of ministry will endure and be rewarded; some works of ministry will not endure. Those who try to do God's work directed by the world's wisdom or with selfish motives will find themselves constructing a flimsy house of straw.

Question 6. This future "Day" is a reference to the judgment seat of Christ (Rom 14:10-12; 2 Cor 5:10). This is not a judgment to determine if a person is saved or lost. We are saved by God's grace through faith alone. The judgment seat will be a time of evaluation of each believer and how that believer has built his or her section of God's building. Our motives, our methods, our faithfulness and our obedience will all be evaluated, and we will be rewarded or lose the reward based on the outcome.

Question 7. The rewards for faithful service are often called "crowns" in the New Testament—visible symbols of victory and endurance that believers will receive from Christ and that we will ultimately lay before God in gratitude and humility (Rev 4:10-11). Rewards are also pictured in Scripture as the Master's declaration of "Well done, good and faithful servant" and as expanded privileges and responsibilities in God's kingdom (Matt 25:21). Group members may have other ways of envisioning Christ's rewards.

Question 8. Paul stresses that loss of reward does not mean loss of salvation. Even the person who is left with nothing after the evaluation of his life "will be saved" (v. 15). Christians who have failed to serve the Lord faithfully will be shown what rewards they could have received had they built differently. A believer's loss of reward will bring a sense of shame (1 Jn 2:28) that will be removed when God wipes every tear from our eyes (Rev 21:4).

Question 9. The reality of a future evaluation before Christ makes some Christians fearful. Remind your group that this is not an evaluation to determine if we are saved or lost, but an evaluation for reward or loss of reward. Paul also says that each believer "will receive his praise from God" (1 Cor 4:5). The purpose of the judgment seat is not condemnation but gracious examination.

We can begin today to build well on our section of God's building and, as a result, we can anticipate that Day when we will hear Jesus tell us, "Well done."

Prayer suggestion. Encourage the members of the group to sit quietly before the Lord and to let him search their lives. We don't have to wait for that future Day of evaluation to know what Jesus thinks of the quality of our work for him. God the Spirit will reveal what pleases him and what is not pleasing to him in our lives right now if we will listen and obey.

Study 6. Fighting the Battle. Ephesians 6:10-18.
Purpose: To make us aware of both the spiritual battle against us and the resources God provides for us to use in fighting that battle.

Group discussion. Possible alternate question: Tell the group about a battle scene from a movie (or from personal experience) that is memorable to you. What stands out in your memory about it?

Question 1. It's possible that some members of the group may struggle with the idea that personal evil forces like Satan and demons really exist. You may want to point out that Jesus and every New Testament writer affirm the reality of Satan and evil beings called demons. In this passage Paul makes it clear that these beings are spiritual, not physical, but they are just as real as anything physical. Furthermore, these evil beings are powerful and set against Jesus and those who follow him. We also learn that Satan has a host of evil beings under his control. Satan is not present everywhere as God is. He must work through other beings who obey his evil will.

Question 2. Evil beings use a variety of methods to attack believers. The attack may come through other people, through a sense of discouragement, or through obstacles and difficulties thrown in our way. Reminding us of past sins is a favorite tactic. The goal of the attack is to defeat us or deceive us or destroy us in some way.

Questions 3-4. The Christian is called to "be strong in the *Lord*" and to not rely on his or her own wisdom or strength to overcome the enemy. Jesus will never forsake us or abandon us, so he is always ready to help. You might want to discuss exactly how we can rely on the Lord in times of spiritual stress (through prayer, through appropriate passages of

Scripture, by calling on Christian friends for support and wisdom). John Stott's words summarize this truth well: "Only the power of God can defend and deliver us from the might, the evil and the craft of the devil. True, the principalities and powers are strong, but the power of God is stronger" (*God's New Society: The Message of Ephesians* [Downers Grove, Ill.: InterVarsity Press, 1980], p. 266).

Question 5. A believer who is not reading and obeying God's Word or who is neglecting to spend time in prayer or who is not recognizing their need for God's power in their life is going to be more vulnerable to Satan's attacks. If Christians become entangled with aspects of the old life they become targets of attack as well. But even men and women who are walking close to the Lord in obedience and faith (like Paul!) can find themselves the objects of Satan's schemes.

Question 6. The protection God provides is pictured by Paul as pieces of armor. The individual pieces seem to illustrate different aspects of spiritual strength that are available to each of us. We are responsible, however, to "put on" the armor—to personally appropriate and use the spiritual resources that God makes available to us.

Question 7. Paul points to the six major pieces of a Roman soldier's equipment and uses them as illustrations of the truth, righteousness, good news of peace, faith, salvation and Word of God that equip us to fight against the enemy's attacks.

The belt of truth (or integrity) provides a sense of inner strength and confidence just as a soldier's wide belt holds his tunic and armor in place.

The breastplate of righteousness (meaning the righteousness of Christ given to us in salvation) protects our vital organs from the slanderous attacks of the enemy. In other words, God's righteous covering protects our inner being—our heart, our spirit—from Satan, who seeks to raise doubts in our minds about our salvation and tries to discourage us from faithfully following the Lord.

Heavy-soled sandals keep a soldier from slipping or sliding. In the same way, the message of the gospel provides a firm place to stand when the enemy attacks. We can rest on its truth. Our peace *with* God and a sense of peace *from* God keep us from falling into unbelief or disobedience.

The shield of faith lays hold of God's promises and declarations about who he is so the believer can put out the flaming arrows of fear or doubt or rebellion.

The helmet of salvation guards our minds by giving us an assurance of our salvation in Christ. The lies and doubts and deceit that Satan wants to plant in our mind are repelled by God's clear promises of our forgiveness and cleansing in Jesus.

The sword is the only offensive weapon at our disposal. God's Word is used to drive the enemy away by exposing his lies and schemes.

Question 8. Prayer is to pervade and cover all our spiritual warfare. Even putting on God's armor is an expression of our total dependence on the Lord. The prayer Paul urges upon us is prayer "in the Spirit"— prayer prompted and guided by the Spirit. Principalities and powers are defeated by the soldier on his knees.

Study 7. Becoming a Servant. John 13:1-17.

Purpose: To impress on us that servanthood is an essential part of following Jesus.

Question 1. Allow the members of the group to "paint the scene" with their descriptions. What tensions would have been evident? How might emotions have been expressed? Then ask them to share how they would have felt being there and having Jesus come to them to wash their feet. Let each person speak without judgment from the group.

Question 2. It was customary in Jesus' day for people to remove their sandals and to rinse the dust from their feet before entering a home. Usually a servant was stationed at the door to carry out that task; always jars of water and towels were provided. If no servant was present, it was social custom for someone in the group to wash the feet of the others. In this passage, none of the disciples was willing to stoop to such a lowly and (in their minds) demeaning job.

Question 3. Jesus knew that his ministry on earth was coming to an end and that he would soon be exalted to the glory he had shared with the Father. He also knew that Judas was his betrayer. In spite of the full understanding he had of his position and destiny, Jesus was willing to take the place of a servant in ministry to others—even ministry to his betrayer.

Question 4. Jesus' goal was to express the depths of his love for his disciples (v. 1). He also wanted to provide a model for their relationship with each other. Jesus' actions demonstrate that leadership in God's kingdom requires a willingness to serve others. Even though Jesus would soon return to the place of exaltation with the Father (v. 3), he willingly assumed the role of a servant. Those of us who want to follow Jesus are called to follow him down a path of sacrifice and self-denial.

Question 5. Peter's strong reaction may have come from a sense of shame because he had not been willing to wash Jesus' feet when they entered the home. It's also probable that Peter wasn't very comfortable seeing Jesus humble himself in such a manner. Another reason for his reaction is that he didn't understand the significance of what Jesus was doing; Peter took the washing of his feet literally.

Jesus explained that the literal foot washing was a picture of Peter's spiritual cleansing. Once the believer has been cleansed from sin by God's grace, all that is needed is daily cleansing from the defilement of the world. Once Peter understood that, he was more than willing to participate.

Question 6. Christians generally see Jesus' example as symbolic of how we are to serve each other in humility. To help cultivate this attitude, some Christians practice literal foot washing as part of their worship. It's possible that the apostles practiced foot washing among themselves after this to be reminded that Jesus alone was Lord and Master and that they were his servants.

Being a servant, however, does not necessarily mean that you do the lowliest tasks. The true servant uses his or her gifts in the role where they are most effective. The leader is to focus on the task of leadership, but the servant leader is also *willing* to serve others in whatever capacity is needed.

Study 8. Entering a Kingdom. Hebrews 12:14-29.
Purpose: To discover what it means to be a citizen of Christ's kingdom.
Background. This passage in Hebrews refers to several Old Testament people and events that may or may not be familiar to members of your study group. It might help you as the leader to read the relevant passages and to have some familiarity with the Old Testament references.

• Esau's trade for his birthright—Genesis 25:29-34

• Moses' reception of the law on Mount Sinai—Exodus 19:10-25; Deuteronomy 4:11-13; 5:22-27

• The blood of Abel—Genesis 4:1-10

• Prophecy of the shaking of the heavens and the earth—Haggai 2:6-7

Question 1. The word *holiness* carries the idea of separation—separation from sin and separation to God. God is holy, and the Bible's call to holiness is a call to purity and integrity. We are to be light as God is light with no darkness in us. Holiness is reflected in actions ("see that no one is sexually immoral") and in attitudes ("no bitter root"; not being "godless" [having no regard for God]).

Question 2. Making an effort to live at peace with all people does not mean that we compromise God's truth or his standards of right living in order to bring peace. It does mean that Christians are to take the initiative to restore and reconcile damaged relationships.

Question 3. The author of Hebrews wants to contrast the experience of Israel's reception of the law with the Christian's experience of receiving God's grace and forgiveness. It might help to have a white board or poster board ready so you can make a chart based on the group's responses to this question.

The second part of question 3 emphasizes the point of these verses. Do we want to live under the gloom and storm of the law or do we want to follow Jesus into the joyful liberation of God's grace?

Question 4. This question provides the opportunity to talk about our motivation for living the Christian life. We do not live a life of purity in order to obey the external threat of the law. We live a holy life in joyful response to God's abundant grace to us. In deciding whether to engage in a certain amusement, for example, we don't consult a Christian "rule book" to see if it is permitted or not. Instead we ask ourselves if this activity pleases the Lord. Would I be embarrassed to ask Jesus to join me? Does what I'm about to do or see or experience strengthen my faith and testimony to others—or does it weaken them? It's not a matter of being pious but a matter of pleasing the One who saved us by his grace.

Question 5. The writer of Hebrews gives us a glimpse into those who inhabit heaven—those with whom some day we will enjoy the glories of heaven. The emphasis is not on the *beauty* of heaven or the *activities* of heaven as much as the *relationships* we will experience in heaven with angels, with believers and (best of all) with Jesus.

Question 6. In spite of the clear contrasts between the burden of the law and the liberation of grace, some Christians are tempted to return to a life governed by rules and traditions rather than a life guided by the Spirit of God. Others may be tempted to turn away from obedience and return to the behaviors of the old life. The writer of Hebrews warns us that the time will come when the created universe will be shaken and removed. Only those who have believed in Jesus and have continued in faith to the end will remain forever.

Question 7. No matter what happens in our world—rising energy costs, economic downturns, natural disasters, war—the Christian can find security and peace in the unshakable kingdom of God. We may lose everything we possess, including life itself, but God and his promises stand firm forever. Nothing on earth can separate us from God, and our eternity with him is secure as well.

Question 8. Christians are in the process of receiving this kingdom from God. We haven't seen it yet in its fullness, but we have tasted its goodness and we anticipate its richness. Our response is to thank and worship God with reverence and awe. This question gives you and your group a chance to do that. God's promises and his wondrous character should bring us to our faces before him.

Question 9. Worship gives us an opportunity to focus on the awesome majesty and glory of God. He is our Savior and Friend and Helper, but he is also the sovereign Ruler of the universe. Occasionally, Christians need to fall before the Lord in adoration and wonder.

The awesome majesty of God also prompts us to take his Word and his truth seriously. What God has spoken cannot be treated lightly.

Question 10. You might want to remind the group of each of the images that you have studied together and how each one pictured a different aspect of what it means to follow Jesus. Encourage each person to talk about one specific image and how it has affected their Christian journey.

Douglas Connelly is senior pastor at Parkside Community Church in Michigan as well as a writer and speaker. His books include The Bible for Blockheads *and* The Book of Revelation for Blockheads *(both by Zondervan). He is also the author of a number of LifeGuide Bible studies.*

What Should We Study Next?

A good place to continue your study of Scripture would be with a book study. Many groups begin with a Gospel such as *Mark* (20 studies by Jim Hoover) or *John* (26 studies by Douglas Connelly). These guides are divided into two parts so that if twenty or twenty-six weeks seems like too much to do at once, the group can feel free to do half and take a break with another topic. Later you might want to come back to it. You might prefer to try a shorter letter. *Philippians* (9 studies by Donald Baker), *Ephesians* (11 studies by Andrew T. and Phyllis J. Le Peau) and *1 & 2 Timothy and Titus* (11 studies by Pete Sommer) are good options. If you want to vary your reading with an Old Testament book, consider *Ecclesiastes* (12 studies by Bill and Teresa Syrios) for a challenging and exciting study.

There are a number of interesting topical LifeGuide studies as well. Here are some options for filling three or four quarters of a year:

Basic Discipleship
Christian Beliefs, 12 studies by Stephen D. Eyre
Christian Character, 12 studies by Andrea Sterk & Peter Scazzero
Christian Disciplines, 12 studies by Andrea Sterk & Peter Scazzero
Evangelism, 12 studies by Rebecca Pippert & Ruth Siemens

Building Community
Fruit of the Spirit, 9 studies by Hazel Offner
Spiritual Gifts, 8 studies by R. Paul Stevens
Christian Community, 10 studies by Rob Suggs

Character Studies
David, 12 studies by Jack Kuhatschek
New Testament Characters, 10 studies by Carolyn Nystrom
Old Testament Characters, 12 studies by Peter Scazzero
Women of the Old Testament, 12 studies by Gladys Hunt

The Trinity
Meeting God, 12 studies by J. I. Packer
Meeting Jesus, 13 studies by Leighton Ford
Meeting the Spirit, 10 studies by Douglas Connelly

OTHER LIFEGUIDE® BIBLE STUDIES
BY DOUGLAS CONNELLY

Angels
Daniel
Elijah
Encountering Jesus
Forgiveness
Good & Evil
Heaven
I Am
John
The Lord's Prayer
Meeting the Spirit
Miracles